Pagans

The origins of the Celts have been put at many dates – everything from 1000 to 350 BC. They inhabited Switzerland or Central Europe before expanding into Gaul, or France, where they were conquered by Julius Caesar, according to his *Gallic Wars*, which records conquests in the broader sphere of the Roman Empire. Julius Caesar and the future emperors of Rome were, of course, also pagans, but not so obsessed with paganism as the Celts, who were steeped in magic and the observance of ritual – more so than anyone else in the old world. The Celts were not observers of a religion with a pantheon like the Roman one. As with most other country-dwellers of the time, the Celts believed that magical agencies pervaded many aspects of their lives and surroundings. They were concerned to use magic for beneficent ends, and they recited myths which were committed to memory. Many believe their myths, cults and sacred terminology sprang from an Indo-European origin, which the Celts shared with the Aryan ancestors of the Hindus and with the Italic forerunners of the Romans.

There is a considerable volume of material written about the Celts, thanks to the Roman historians, despite much church expurgation in the ancient literature of Ireland. Many mythical tracts point to deities, the main pagan festivals, the activities of the Druids and other related matters.

The Roman historians and generals wrote in Latin, and seldom in Greek, the works being dedicated to a local god. The monuments, normally altars of a purely Roman type, provide an iconography where none existed, or hardly so, in these ancient times. Julius Caesar's *Gallic Wars* and other classical works provide a soldier's view of the Celts that threatened the Roman Empire in the closing years BC.

On the Druids, and on various beliefs reported of the Celts, Greek and Roman sources have more useful information. Information can also be gleaned from the philosophers of the Celts and in the study of Celtic place names, and sites connected with the Celts. There is archaeological evidence of burial sites and votive offerings at sacred sites like the oak groves of the Druids and their temples along with the colleges where Druids trained. Some Gaulish and British coins have been found at such sites from immediately before Julius Caesar's conquest of Gaul.

It is useful to look at the life of the ordinary Celt to form a judgement of the role they played in ancient times. They lived for the rural festivals, four of which were held at turning points in the year; there were the warm and cold festivals. In Ireland the greatest festival was Samhain, celebrated in terms of the modern calendar on 1 November.

Contents

Also from Michael Sheane

Ulster & Its Future After the Troubles (1977)
Ulster & The German Solution (1978)
Ulster & The British Connection (1979)
Ulster & The Lords of the North (1980)
Ulster & The Middle Ages (1982)
Ulster & St Patrick (1984)
The Twilight Pagans (1990)
Enemy of England (1991)
The Great Siege (2002)
Ulster in the Age of Saint Comgall of Bangor (2004)
Ulster Blood (2005)
King William's Victory (2006)
Ulster Stock (2007)
Famine in the Land of Ulster (2008)
Pre-Christian Ulster (2009)
The Glens of Antrim (2010)
Ulster Women – A Short History (2010)
The Invasion of Ulster (2010)
Ulster in the Viking Age (2011)
Ulster in the Eighteenth Century (2011)
Ulster in the History of Ireland (2012)
Rathlin Island (2013)
Saint Patrick's Missionary Journeys in Ireland (2015)
The Story of Carrickfergus (2015)
Ireland's Holy Places (2016)
The Conqueror of the North (2017)
The Story of Holywell Hospital: A Country Asylum (2018)
Patrick: A Saint for All Seasons (2019)
The Picts: The Painted People (2019)
Pictland: The Conversion to Christianity of a Pagan Race (2020)
Irish & Scottish Dalriada (2020)
The Roman Empire (2021)
The Ancient Picts of the Scottish Highlands of the Seventh Century (2021)

The Celtic Supernatural

The Ritual Year

The night before 1 November was the most significant night – what we call Halloween. Samhain marked the end of one year and the start of the next. It was considered to stand independently between the two years, and its position in relation to the natural seasons shows that it was the turning point in a pastoralist rather than an agrarian cycle. It corresponds to the time when grazing herds and flocks were assembled, and only those animals required for breeding were spared from slaughter. This was an age-old custom, dating back in temperate Europe to the Neolithic farmers. It was a time for unlimited feasting.

The word 'Samhain' appears to mean an assembly or gathering together, and in Ireland the tribal region (*tuatha*) may be seen as reuniting at this time. In the literature of a later period the importance of this festival was so great that nearly everything ascribed to the pre-Christian calendar took place at Samhain, but its real magical significance was its connection with the renewal of earthly prosperity and tribal success, the germination of good fortune for the coming spring and summer. Samhain was concerned with the renewal of the fecundity of the earth and its people.

The god Dagda mated with the goddess Morrigan, or with

Boann, the deity of the River Boyne. The name 'Dagda' meant the good god – not in the sense of being morally good, but in the sense of being competent at all things. He is the father of the tribe, and its benefactor. But there were no comparable gods for war, wisdom or maybe even the sun. There are many gods known throughout the Celtic Empire.

The Dagda mated at Samhain, as has been mentioned, with a nature goddess, Morrigan, Queen of Demons. She is mentioned frequently in Irish or Gaelic texts, but her name is interchangeable with those of other horrific deities, such as Nem (Panic), and Badl Catha (Raven of Battle); and others, like Macha, appear upon the scene. The Celtic goddess, in fact, represents a general type, not tribal or social, for they are of the land or territory to be placated, taken over or enslaved. They display fertility and other characteristics, and may be symbolised in the sun and moon no less than in zoomorphism and topography.

These, then, were the supernatural powers to be placated at Samhain. The night before Samhain was a time when the earth was overrun by magical forces, a time when demons issued forth from caves and mounds, and individuals might be received into these realms, a time when monsters assailed the royal strongholds with flames and poison.

The second most important festival in Ireland, or Eirinn, was that of 1 May, the start of the warm season. Known as Beltane or Cetshamain, it was also a pastoralist festival, corresponding to when the cattle would be driven to open grazing. Great fires burned on this occasion, continuing well into Christian times, and the Druids supervised the driving of cattle between two fires to protect them from disease. The word 'Beltane' is perhaps connected with a god's name – Belenus, a very ancient God.

The other lesser festivals in ancient Ireland were Imbolc, on 1 February, and Lugnasad, on 1 August. Less is known about Imbolc. Imbolc marked the beginning of the lactation of the ewes, and corresponded to the feast of St Bridget in the Christian calendar. The goddess Bridget can also be traced back in Europe to place names and inscriptions. The festival of Imbolc may also have been connected to the tending of sheep, for the working of wool was important in Celtic economies.

The Lugnasad festival was introduced later by a number of tribes coming to Ireland. This festival appears to be the most agrarian in character of those known in Ireland. Its date, 1 August, was when the practice of transhumance was in full swing. It was also connected with the ripening of the crops, and later, in Christian times, it was associated with the harvest service. It has also been associated with the god Lug, who appears to have been a latecomer among Irish divine beings. He was a tribal god, and he is portrayed as lord of every skill and all knowledge of all subjects. Lug appears to have been brought to Ireland by Gaulish settlers, perhaps in the first century BC. There was another name for the August festival – Bron Trograin, which has been interpreted as the Rage of Trograin. During the festival sacrifices were made to the deity for increase and plenty.

The calendar from which these festivals were computed is known in both Irish and classical sources to have been based on lunar observations, and to have counted nights rather than days. The choice of a feast day was also overseen by the Druids. Also, the success of a king's reign was based on the welfare of his tribe. This matter is well exemplified in the Irish texts, and it can be seen that the failure of the crops, cattle disease or other misfortunes might be attributed to the supernatural. A king could be deposed if he developed a physical blemish or a blemish of any other kind.

Some principal aspects of kingship may be discussed here: the king was said to be a mortal mate of the territorial goddess. The goddess had given them the goblet, symbolic of marriage in Celtic society; the bride would await her husband at a nearby well. The Tara High Kingship stories are much concerned with instancing perfect reigns, in which there were plentiful harvests and other welcome conditions. As the King aged so his realm might suffer a decline. There is little doubt that a Celtic king might have a sticky end – perhaps death by drowning or burning, in the midst of high magic, in the presence of the tribal god.

Tribal and Nature Deities

In the stories connected with Samhain, the Dagda is represented as a grotesque figure of immense strength and appetites. He is clad in the garments of a servant. His weapon is a great club, sometimes dragged on wheels, and he sports a magic cauldron which provides inspiration. The great chalk-cut figure of a naked man wielding a club must represent such a god. The Dagda has been depicted with a hammer and a cup or dish which may be the counterpart of the cauldron.

The symbol of abundance in Ireland is a magical cauldron. Of the Dagda it was said that none went away without being satisfied, but vessels such as the cauldron associated with other Irish or Gaelic gods, such as those in Munster, were used for brewing immortal beer.

The tribal cauldron played its part in the deaths of kings. The grotesque male figure appears in a number of other Irish mythological stories, and in Welsh literature one emerges from a lake with his cauldron and his wife. In contrast the god Lug is always portrayed as a young man, and is a representative of a primitive concept. The transfiguration of the goddess from maiden to hag is outlined in the stories. They appeared as ferocious warriors on the battlefield. The famous Ulster hero

Cuchulain was confronted by Badb attired in a red cloak and with red eyebrows mounted in a chariot or cart drawn by ugly horses. There was much horror.

The Badl Catha, the Raven of Battle, introduces the zoomorphic aspect – a trait of many Celtic deities of both sexes. The evidence shows that deities in human form had been long known among Indo-European peoples. The male deities seem less markedly zoomorphic than the female, but the name Lug may mean a lynx, and in Europe he was also known by other names in the first century BC. The horse does not play an important role in the names of male deities, although in Ireland there were mythological horses. Horse symbolism is most closely attached to a goddess, and the most widespread horse-related goddess was Epona, pictured on many Gallo-Roman altars. Some believe Epona is equivalent to Macha of County Armagh in Ulster.

Another aspect of the Celtic deities, male and female, is 'triplism' – a matter explored in much detail. It is the union of three supernatural beings, the number three being sacred (For example, the Christian Trinity). It is interesting that Celtic deities are grouped in accordance with the sex of the deity and the triads take various forms – as between Morrigan and other deities. Triads of goddesses in Ireland are mirrored in the many Gallo-Roman dedications to mothers. Triads of male deities in Ireland also take many forms, but the main characters, such as the Dagda and Lug, are not strikingly triple.

From Roman Gaul are known three-headed, or three-faced, sculptures of a native god. Another horrific member of the supernatural world is Ellen Trechend, who issued from the cave of Cruachain and devastated Ireland. The three gods of skill do not appear to have any direct mortal connections, at least in the same forms. They played a role in the supernatural world.

Gods would surround the Celts as they went about hunting, as recorded in the account of the three sons of the Kings of Iruath. The *fiana* devoted themselves to hunting and warfare, which was typical of many Irish people.

Supernatural Kingdoms

Was there some kind of Celtic pantheon? In Ireland the answer to this question revolves around the nature of the Tuatha de Danann, a title that may be interpreted as 'the people of the goddess Danu'. The Celts brewed magical beer when they went into battle, to protect them against the powers of ill-intent and misfortune. This custom appears to have had a long history. It may not have had a bearing on the tribal cult, but concerned the magico-religious men of learning.

A look at the Indo-European divine society reveals the specialization of the gods according to their function, or attribute, as is the case with Mars, Mercury and Jupiter. These gods were mostly Mediterranean and urban, unknown to the Celts before the Roman conquests. Such gods and goddesses were strictly supernatural magicians, themselves requiring magic for their own continuance. As far as the Tuatha de Danann is concerned, a political confederation of many tribes would have led to the emergence of a paramount tribe whose gods would most likely have been considered to take into clientage the gods of subjected peoples. This phenomenon may be indicated in the iconography of some Gaulish monuments, and a good case may be made for its operation amongst the Tuatha de Danann.

Gallo-Roman Monuments

Let us take a look at the Roman monuments in Gaul and the Rhineland to learn a little about the iconography in which these deities were portrayed, and how they were matched with Roman gods.

Caesar was concerned about perpetuating accurate information about the Celtic gods. The names of a large number of local Celtic deities are recorded on Roman monuments, and Mars stands out. Lucan, writing in the first century ad, gives prominence to three Celtic gods – Tarinus, Teutantes and Esus, these names being quite obscure. The general applicability of the Celtic names is evident. These were the gods of thunder and people.

Many dedications incorporating names of Celtic deities can be found on altars or votive tablets without iconography, but there are also a number of deity representations. Principal amongst these figures are three-headed or three-faced gods. One depiction is of squatting gods, one with a snake, one with a wheel or mounted on a horse supported by a giant. A three-headed god can be seen in the lands of the Belgae; others are in France in the Massif Central and the Lower Rhine Valley, and also in the Champagne region. The tendency was to Romanize Celtic deities. There is no doubt, however, that there was a mingling of names in regard to deities. In the territory of one God there were many godly dedications, and others might be added.

The main source of material comes from Gaul, and inscriptions seem restricted to a few regions with military connections. They include Welsh gods, not recorded in other epigraphy. There are also interesting remains in the area of Hadrian's Wall. Regarding these monuments and inscriptions of Roman times in Gaul and Britain, the more recent they are the less trustworthy they are for regional investigation. The movement of auxiliary troops and individuals across the English Channel was such that deity transplantations were not infrequent.

Native Iconography

As mentioned previously, the Romanization of native cults shows that a selection of seemingly standardized monuments was largely employed. This is not to deny that the symbols of horses, wheels and so on were also in use in the days before the Roman conquest of Gaul. But these things cannot be dismissed as borrowings from the Mediterranean iconography, however much their presentation was influenced from that quarter. Most of the pre-Roman images were made out of wood and have not survived; but that some were recognizably anthropomorphic seems likely, for their powers were often assigned by Caesar to the god Mercury.

In Northern Europe, and in Britain and Ireland, the peat has preserved many wooden objects and a number of images of the Bronze Age. There are a number of La Tène-style masks and heads, and heads of figures on Celtic coins. It must have been largely a matter of available craftsmanship, and it was only in rare cases that images of stone or bronze could be achieved. The hazards of the intervening centuries have of course reduced the possibility of appreciating the significance of such creations.

Amongst the many types of representation mentioned before in Gaul or France, the squatting figure perhaps dates back to the second century BC. It is found in the monumental sculpture of, for example, the great sanctuaries near Aix-en-Provence. Some of them were destroyed by the Romans in 124 BC. These places cannot be regarded as typical of Celtic practice, for they lie in the area most open to the influence of Mediterranean civilization, whether in the sphere of colonial Greek Massilia or the Graeco-Etruscan sphere of Northern Italy. At most, the Celtic element around the Lower Rhône was composed of warrior overlords, and their culture was that of their Ligurian subjects and their more civilized neighbours.

The other sanctuaries in the same region may have elements of Celtic symbolism and ritual. The outline friezes of horses and carved birds, and niches for the showing of human heads, agree with the kind of symbolism derived from more primitive regions. The large human stone sculptures at Roquepertuse sit cross-legged with the lower legs drawn close to the hips and the soles of the feet turned upwards. This has appeared as something very oriental to many writers, but it was perhaps the normal ground-sitting posture amongst the Celts, as it remains with many Asiatic peoples. Here was something of the Eurasiatic way of life forsaken in the West on the general adoption of chairs and stools. This pose may have been appropriate in rituals concerning gods and devotees, whether receiving or offering gifts, or in rituals concerning the recitation of sacred texts.

The attire of the Roquepertuse figures, with the exception of a square-cut cape, consisting of a small tunic gathered at the waist with a belt, illustrates that this type of clothing was more than a century in advance of Diodorus Siculus. In the absence of immediate examples of cult art in Gaul between the Roquepertuse statuary and the various Gallo-Roman pieces, it is hard to say what influence, if any, the southern sanctuaries may have had on northern areas. It is not likely that the squatting pose was always propagated from that quarter.

An earlier, and maybe more potent, exotic influence in Celtic cult art was that of the Etruscans, and this can be seen in the Middle Rhenish Zone. Here, motifs of Etruscan origin are shown in sculpture wholly Celtic in general composition. This evidence is important in showing the extent to which ideas about sacred monuments may have developed at a time when the Celts were at their most receptive. The relief-carved four-sided pillar from Pfalzfeld is the most impressive of these existing monuments with a Celtic significance. Its essential character is that of a tapering monolith decorated on all sides with floriate motifs in the early La Tène style. In the midst of each panel peered forth a human face surmounted by a carved head, but this has disappeared within recent centuries. There is no other comparable pillar. On stylistic grounds, taking into account Etruscan influence north of the Alps, the Pfalzfeld pillar should date to within the fourth century BC, if not a little earlier. It represents a sacred tree or the epitome of a tribal deity.

Sacred Matters

At a much later date is a type of Gallo-Roman monument not hitherto mentioned – the so-called Jupiter Column, named after the god and planet. Monuments of this type have their own main distribution in the Middle Rhenish Zone, both east and west, and extend into the Vosges with a wide dispersal in North Eastern and Central Gaul. The overall appearance of these monuments is Roman. They consist of a square base surmounted by a swelling and slightly tapering column, with a capital, surmounted in turn by a sculptured device. The base, and even the column, is often decorated with figures of Roman gods, but the topmost element portrays a device more at home in native cults. This usually is a sculptured horseman and emergent giant who supports the horse's front feet. The rider, with a beard, is in Roman military attire, but may have a waterwheel as well as weapons. In some cases a seated male figure, or a male-and-female couple, takes the place of an equestrian group. All these subjects can be reconciled with the general theme of the all-purpose Celtic gods already expounded.

But it is not the iconography that is of great interest, but the column itself. Its prevalence within the Middle Rhenish Zone suggests that it had native forerunners in wood and, again, that its protype was the growing sacred tree. It appears that Gallo-Roman epigraphy, and depictions of Irish oaks, throws some light on the role of the sacred trees amongst the Celts. Gods of oak and beech are known from dedications. The tribal name 'Eburones' incorporates the word for yew, and Gaulish proper names include 'Guidgen', son of wood, and 'Guergen', son of alder.

In Ireland there are a number of allusions to a sacred tree (*bile*), and this word can be compared with the French place name 'Billom', the plain, or clearing, of the sacred tree. Again, Irish mythological names, such as Mac Cuilinn, son of Holly, and Mac Ibar, son of yew, tell a similar story. The Middle Rhenish Celts may be credited with adopting for their own use the Etruscan practice of raising sculptured stone monuments, and it may be from this quarter that they received the idea of portraying two-headed, or two-faced, Janus-like images.

The finest surviving example of a tall stone is in Germany. It shows the two opposing sides of a shallow-cut human face with a right forearm extending across the body. This figure also appears to have had a leaf crown standing free, shared by the two faces. The Hozgerlingen stone has no ornamental carving, and the emphasis is upon the face. There is no real side view, or profile. It is likely that these and related stones were set up in shrines or statuaries of a type to be seen later.

One of the most arresting pieces from Roquepertuse is a Janus composition of two heads, and this may reinforce the view that the River Rhône is significant in the history of cult art in the central Celtic area. The ritual interest of these heads is apparent in the faces on the Pfalzfeld pillar, which look in four directions. This underlines the superhuman nature of the deity, and the purely Celtic embodiment of this, involving the sacred number three, would have been a later sculptural development.

Finally, an even more interesting stone, of an earlier date, deserves mention. It was found at Srockkach, near Tubingen, in association with a cremation burial under a tumulus. The grave offerings belong to the Hallstatt iron-using culture. The stone, which was broken, shows a head with a single face. The shoulders are marked but there is no neck, and the only other feature is a single zigzag line running round all sides beneath the shoulders. It is perhaps unnecessary to seek southern origins for this piece.

Sacred Enclosures

The precincts of sacred trees and other objects of veneration are now to be considered. Except for sanctuaries such as Roquepertuse and Entremont, lying in more important places, the sacred places of the Celts prior to, or beyond, the Roman Empire appear to have been of the simplest kind. A widespread form appears to have been a sacred wood, or piece of ground upon which stood groves of trees. This seems to be the general implication of the word 'nemeton', which is widely known throughout the Celtic lands. There are a number of examples of this in Asia Minor. In Britain there was a place called Vernemeton, in Nottinghamshire. In Ireland, *fidnemed* meant a sacred wood. It may also have meant a sacred enclosure. There are also mentions of the Druids and the sacred groves where they performed their sacrifices, but the Celtic word in question is not mentioned in the ancient writings. There is no evidence that these sacred sites were used as places of burial; nor are there any remains from other Iron Age shrines. There is also to be considered the testimony of native-style temples erected during the time of Roman rule, although one may indeed house ancestral tombs while others can be shown to have no funerary connections.

Celtic Shrines

The site at Filford consisted of six large post holes in two close lines of three each. The form of the original enclosure is not known. From a later date there are the remains of a horseshoe-shaped arrangement of uprights, but it cannot be proven that they were there to support a roof. They may have enclosed a site of veneration.

Early in the Romanization of the district, the site was dismantled and levelled, and a circular stone-built wall was erected in its place. It is not known what kind of structure, if any, this wall supported, but evidence of a fire in later Roman times suggests that by then there was a wooden superstructure – maybe a roof – in position. It is clear that the Iron Age shrine continued to be held in respect, but the Roman 'rotunda' should perhaps be regarded as the culmination of this at a time when the real centre of the cult had shifted to the temple a short distance away. This Romano-British temple was of a simple construction. It was of the square-built type that will be described presently.

The site of Saint-Margarethaen-am-Silberberg, dating perhaps from the early first century BC, indicates a circular post-built hut some twenty feet in diameter, probably covered with a conical thatched roof. It cannot be shown that this was a more ancient house than the rectangular ones at the same site. It, however, seems to have resembled the round native temples in the Celtic areas of the Roman Empire. It may also have some resemblance to those mythological feasting halls that play an important part in some Irish kinship stories. These too were perhaps round in plan.

An interesting site known as Goloring lies in the Kobener Wald, between Koblenz and Mayen. It was excavated in recent years. Here there is a circular area some 600 feet in diameter, enclosed by a bank and an inner ditch. In the centre is an enclosed elevated area some 120 feet high and some 290 feet across. At its centre was found a hole which once held a wooden post of great height – possibly of the order of forty feet. Excavations revealed that a long ramp had led into the hole on one side, and this may have been used for sliding in the foot of the post, which would have been levered and hauled upright into position. This was the normal procedure in ancient Europe for tipping large stones upright, and the technique was well known in Neolithic Britain.

There is no evidence of burial and habitation at Goloring, but potsherds in the composition of the central area, and in the ditch silting, indicate construction in late Hallstatt times, and therefore possibly in the sixth century BC. Goloring is now covered in trees, but it stood in open country, and its situation was towards the southern side of a low ridge. The standing post would have been a conspicuous landmark for some distance around. It may have been the site of a tribal assembly. Here there was adequate space for a concourse with its assertions of rights, deliberations, judgments, games and marketing.

Funerary associations were not lacking, for close by were two groups of tumuli dating from Urnfield to Hallstatt times. No other site of this kind has been excavated on the continent.

The general nature of Goloring seems to indicate that it was part of the Rhenish Zone, and it seems to compare with royal sites of assembly in places in Ireland – for example, Tara, Emain Macha (in County Armagh) and Knockaulin (in County Kildare). At all of these earthworks there are ramparts – effective for defence where the earthwork was on sloping ground. Analogies to the standing post at Goloring are not as yet known in Ireland, but stone pillars, memorials and gravestones are easy to observe, so it is likely that the relationship between the Goloring and Irish earthworks will be seen in a clearer light in future. In Ireland the juxtaposition, at the main place of assembly, of various kinds of enclosures and burial mounds stresses the importance of ancestral tombs. A reference to the rightness of assembly at funerary monuments can be seen in the Senchus Mor, a legal document dating from the eighth century AD.

As yet no Irish site has revealed tombs that can be considered as those of founder settlers or immediate ancestors of the Irish Celts, but this may be largely a matter of further excavation. At Tara, the Celtic traditions were adapted to a hilltop that had already been sanctified for centuries by the presence of an early Bronze Age tomb, and subsequent burials made in its covering mound. This won over the supernatural powers of the countryside, represented chiefly by the nature gods.

At Tara, in Ireland, Medb or Etain might well claim an ancestor in the early Bronze Age tomb goddess, who was of Mediterranean, not of Indo-European, origins. It appears that no overall development should be sought in examining the holy places of the Celts, but the identification of sites showing shrine and burial aspects is interesting. Such sites have been identified in the Department of the Marne, in France. Here square ditch enclosures and burial places were used by families over many centuries. At the site excavated at Ecury-le-Repos, the sides of the square enclosures were about thirty-three feet long, and at the centre of the enclosures were found four large post holes arranged in a rough square with a single large oval post hole at the centre point. Here there may have been a roofed shrine covering a free-standing object, whether a post or a carved image. The oldest burial within the precinct was by inhumation, and it lay immediately west of the shrine; both it and another inhumation in a less privileged position contained brooches of La Tène style. Other burials were by cremation. These, with their pottery, showed a continuous use into Roman times.

Romano-Celtic Temples

The Ecury-le-Repos shrine, with its enclosed ditch, may well be regarded as an antecedent to the most common form of Celtic temple in more durable building material under common encouragement. The essential features of these temples were a small square building and the shrine itself, or cella. The building was entered through a single door, and was usually surrounded by a portico or a veranda. The whole normally stood within a square enclosure. It is clear that the congregation stood outside the temple, but the portico provided a place where images and symbols could be brought out for exposure and veneration. The fact that the portico surrounds all four sides of the shrine may suggest that its function was for processions, which would probably have moved in a sun-wise direction about the temple. Under the shelter of the portico roof may well have sat men reciting the ritual texts appropriate to each festival. At Heathrow, in Middlesex, is an explicit wooden prototype of the pre-Roman Iron Age. These square temples were not places of burial.

In Gaul, or France, the Roman Celtic temple is found in great numbers. They were erected in towns, and at thermal springs and other country places, including some hilltops. At some sites an original pre-Roman tomb and sanctuary appear to have been incorporated, and it has been claimed that the special virtue of these temples lay in the presence of a god or hero ancestor on whom the local people were dependent. The Irish or Gaelic literary evidence all points to tribal ancestry in the genealogies, and to the gods and tombs of mortal heroes in the field monuments.

Another type of monument associated with the Celts here draws our attention. In Central Spain and in Northern Portugal, generally associated with Celtic tribes, are found large stone sculptures of boars and bulls. The inspiration for these sculptures is perhaps Mediterranean, but they perhaps suited Celtic needs, for these figures had to do with the fertility of the herds. The sculptures have been found sited in cattle enclosures beneath the actual citadels. In Northern Portugal there are also sculptures of armed warriors, and these also may have provided a protective force.

Votive Offerings

Perhaps the most spectacular of the Celtic sacred places were those associated with votive offerings that were exposed to full view in the open. Julius Caesar mentions Celtic weapons and other booty heaped on the ground; and these lay unmolested, dedicated to the god of the conquering side in intertribal warfare. One Poseidonius, who travelled in Gaul in the first century BC, is quoted by Strabo regarding the great votive treasure of the Volcae Tectesages which was deposited in sacred enclosures and pools near Tolosa, or Toulouse. This treasure was pillaged by the Romans in 106 BC, and it is reported to have been of unworked gold and silver from which the ingots of these metals had been made up. The reference to the sacred pools by Poseidonius is of much interest in view of the number of finds that may be interpreted as votive deposits. Within the Celtic Iron Age may be cited finds from La Tène itself, from Port and other sites in Switzerland, from Llyn Cerrig Bach in Anglesey, and sites in Scotland.

There are also many interesting finds from peat bogs and rivers that may have been dedicated to the supernatural; and in Northern Europe, beyond the lands of the Celts, there are many interesting votive deposits of actual Celtic objects which also throw some light on the matter. At La Tène, the great accumulation of iron weapons and equipment, including woodwork and a complete wheel, lay in the peat a little offshore in a small bay on the eastern end of the lake of Neucharel. Some human-skeleton remains were also found, and a jetty-like construction had perhaps provided a platform on which the offerings were made.

The discoveries at Port on the Nidau–Burne Canal, at the north-eastern end of Lake Biel, came from an old river. Here the finds have been largely weapons, including spearheads and swords. Some of the swords display punch marks of master swordsmiths, and are in good condition. The remains of a wooden structure were also found at Port.

In Anglesey, at Llyn Cerrig Bach much light has been thrown on the sources and composition of objects in a large votive deposit. The site had been an area of standing water – part of a lake near a rock shelf on the shore. From this vantage point had been thrown many weapons, chariot fittings, slave chains and the remains of some cauldrons, trumpets, and pieces of fine bronze work decorated in the La Tène style. A large number of bones, of ox, horse, sheep, pig and dog, were also found, and these appear to have been sacrificed animals rather than domestic refuse, of which there was no other indication.

The metal objects were dated to between the second century bc and the mid-first century ad. It seems likely that the Llyn Carrig Bach material represents a series of offerings made over a period of time, but its discontinuation in the mid-first century is almost certainly related to the storming of Mona by the Romans in ad 61.

The fine pieces of later date in the deposit come from Britain. They suggest the presence of refugees, and they have been associated with rites to stem the tide of calamity. Three much smaller collections of votive offerings from the first and second centuries ad have been found in Carlingwark and other areas in Scotland. Some of the objects have been found placed in cauldrons for ritualistic reasons. The tools and equipment of native and Roman work were broken and worn out when deposited.

Making offerings of defective objects seems to have been quite in order. Presumably the essence of each piece, rather than its condition, was considered sufficient for it to be associated with the supernatural. These deposits are of wide interest for they were obviously a single act, and made in water in places that were thought to be especially sacred, and therefore suitable for such rights. Not all objects found in water can be described with certainty as single votive offerings; the bronze shield in the late insular La Tène style from the Thames at Battersea, and the later shield and sword from the River Witham in Lincolnshire, have been cited as objects that were perhaps lost when crossing these rivers.

The recovery of votive deposits from waterlogged sites must depend to some extent on geographical factors, including changing water levels and the modern exploitation of peat. This practice of leaving offerings in water or marsh is known to date to the early Neolithic in Denmark, where conditions for preservation have been particularly favourable. The custom appears to have been continuous in pagan times in the Teutonic north, but it is not likely that elsewhere in transalpine Europe votive deposits were made from an early beginning.

Sacrifices

Sacred precincts and votive offerings lead one to ask questions about human and animal sacrifices, and those within the community who were responsible for performing the acts. But it is impossible to establish the sequence of ceremonies pertinent to the various seasonal festivals, and for the contingencies of war, famine and disease. The classical references are too short and vague, and the Irish literary sources relay only indirect information. In the first case such ceremonies were considered too barbarous, and in the second case they were considered too heathenish to merit detailed descriptions.

With regard to the Gaelic or Irish seasonal festivals, it has been said that cattle were sacrificed at Bron Trograin, and there exists much evidence that animals were sacrificed at the festival of Samhain, the start of the Celtic new year. Human sacrifice is referred to in a tale about a maiden that was wooed at Bri Lli by the men of Ireland – for each man that was wooed, one of their people was slain, no one knowing who perpetrated the deed. Bri Lli was another name for Cruachain, the royal centre of the Irish kingdom of Connaught. It appears that the nature goddess's goodwill was secured through the sacrifice of a man from each community. The secret dispatch of the victim, probably using a stabbing weapon, recalls some royal deaths, and the victim's life was in the hands of those in charge of the rites. More general and unlikely allusions to the sacrifice of children and animals at Samhain are to be found in the manuscripts; that these contain an element of truth is likely, but they do not contribute to any closer understanding of the setting.

One of the most important survivals relating to Irish mythology is a reference to the use of sacrifices to readdress misfortunes consequent upon an alliance between a King of Tara and a strange woman. The ritual prescribed by the Druids is the sacrifice of the son of a sinless couple. The account relates the fabulous circumstances of the intended victim's discovery; but once he reached Tara, and was at the point of sacrifice, a supernatural woman appeared leading a cow which she directed to be offered in substitution. This story has a parallel in Aryan tradition in India, pointing to a common heritage, but its significance lies in its implication that Celtic societies practiced the kind of ritual in which an animal could be substituted for a human victim.

The same implication is found in a story featuring an account of a battle that may have been fought in pre-Christian times. In this battle, a race called the Desi overcame the people of Ossory as the result of a Druid having allowed himself to be killed in the form of a cow. Here the sacrifice of one of the most sacred human beings was undertaken to ensure the outcome of the battle, but the gruesomeness of the rite has been ameliorated by means of the magician's supposed shape-shifting prowess.

It is not possible to deduce that human sacrifice had been mostly abandoned for animal offerings among the Irish Celts. Perhaps it took place only in particular situations or among certain peoples, but the evident ritual death of some kings has not been forgotten. The classical evidence for human victims in Gaul and Britain is strong, and to the principal of these we must now turn our attention.

Caesar well understood the nature of sacrifice among the Gauls, but there was nothing extraordinary in this custom in Gaul or in the wider Celtic 'empire'; it was only that the Celts had retained archaic practices in Gaul which in Italy, as in Greece, were by then much outmoded.

It appears that the most usual method of sacrifice was by a stabbing weapon, and sacrifice was followed by the sprinkling of blood on special objects, including altars and trees. This can be learned from Tacitus and Lucan. There was also the divination of auspices by examining human entrails. Of more interest are reports of burnings, drownings and hangings. Early on, Caesar described how some Gaulish tribes made large images out of wickerwork, filled them with living victims, and then set them alight. The victims were said to have been mainly malefactors, and it may be deduced that, whatever actual crimes these persons committed, it did not affect their integrity. It does not appear that captives taken in battle were offered in this way. These sacrifices appear to have ensured tribal welfare, and may have coincided with changes in the Irish Gaelic seasons, four times a year.

The wickerwork containers feature in various Irish stories, many of them mythological. Others tell of houses burned down, and the death of people, sometimes kings, within. Events of this kind are well recorded by Lucan; and the early historian's writings that have survived name three Celtic gods, Teutates, Taranis and Esus. Taranis is said to have been propitiated by drownings, others by hangings. It should be remembered that these three names have been ascribed to Gaulish tribal deities, and the rites may have been attributed to other tribes. It is also possible that these three gods symbolized the elements of earth and vegetation. Sacrifice by drowning is depicted on one of the panels of a large silver basin from Gunderstrup in Denmark, where it was found in a peat bog. In manufacture it was of Celtic origin, dating perhaps from the first century BC, and it came from the Celts settled along the Danube rather than from the Gauls. The account of sacrifice to Esus by hanging is of much interest with its reference to sacred trees. This rite was also practised in honour of Othin, the magician god of the Teutonic barbarians' warrior aristocracy, whose cult was centred in Sweden, and who may have been also of Celtic origin.

Magicians and Sages

Chief among the Celtic magicians were the Druids, but the romantic works describing these magicians were written in later centuries. Comparable religions were found in Europe at this time. Of these, the most outstanding examples are the Brahmins, who continued to feature in Hindu society since the Aryan invasions of India in the mid- or late second millennium bc. The Brahmins have, of course, for some time formed a hereditary caste, but they appear to have been a phenomenon in contemporary society in India. Among the Celts the organization of society included the recruitment of children into the warrior aristocracy. The word '*Drui*' as used in modern-day Europe is derived from continental Celtic through Greek and Latin texts. Julius Caesar wrote about the *Druides* and Cicero of the *Drudae*. These are Latinized forms of the plural.

In surviving insular Celtic languages, *Drui* (singular) *Druae* (plural) are forms of the same word from ancient Gaelic or Irish texts. '*Dryw*' is the Welsh equivalent in the singular. 'Druid' as a word is said to derive from a term used to describe the knowledge of the oak, a sacred tree. The connection between the Druid and the oak is explicit in Pliny's account of the cutting of the mistletoe from the oak by the Druids, and the sacrifice of bulls.

The essence of Druidic knowledge of the supernatural is made clearer by the consideration of other Celtic learned magicians.

As well as Druids and bards, Strabo mentions the *vates*. This word is cognate with the Irish *farhi*. These words spring from a root meaning inspired, and thence prophet or poet. Another Irish term of early Christian times was the *fili*, originally meaning seer, the invisible, but it became the usual name for a poet. Knowledge was a matter of seeing the invisible.

The Druid would fling himself into a trance or a frenzy when a new High King of Ireland was proclaimed by the killing of a bull. The Druid would then gorge on its flesh. Incantations were recited over the Druid, and at length he would give his blessing to the new High King. This title was known as *Tarbfeis*, or Bull Dream.

Trances and frenzies appear to point to some kind of generic connection between the Celtic magician and the shaman of the Northern Eurasiatic zone. Many classical writers have described the Druids as philosophers, and Julius Caesar had a Druid friend. The Druids had their views on the afterlife. The dead, they said, needed weapons, ornaments and food for their journey beyond the grave. The pre-eminence of the Druids in Celtic society is clear from what Caesar and others say about their duties as arbitrators, no less than magicians; and in Ireland their status is best illustrated by the fact that a rí, or king, might not speak until his Druid had first expressed himself. Druids were householders and may have borne arms, but Julius Caesar suggests otherwise so far as fighting was concerned.

Let us now look at the Celtic transmission of learning and literature.

Oral Learning

Modern society is dependent on written literature, so it is perhaps difficult for many people to envisage any other means of conserving knowledge, or a national tradition. Long 'texts' are hard to commit to memory and transmit from one generation to another, but this was the practice among Indo-European peoples lying beyond the bounds of civilization or before writing first came into use.

The mechanism of oral learning is mostly a matter of continuous repetition, made easier by chanting the words in the form of simple verse or alliterative prose. The rhythm may induce a semi-ecstatic state, and over the years a great body of information may be committed to memory. Learning was sacred in the ancient world, and the principle of merit was important. All these aspects are seen in India and in Ireland. But Caesar misunderstood the reason why the Druids did not use writing. It was not just a matter of maintaining secrecy; writing did not have the necessary ritual acceptance – it was not hallowed by ancient usage. Oral learning by nature was conservative, so the everyday spoken language grew farther away from the learned tongue. The great example of this is the language of the Vedic hymns, which is earlier than the Sanskrit in which the commentaries on them came to be taught. But Sanskrit itself was a language of the learned. These texts were conserved over a millennium in India, and were not written down until the eighteenth century, when some of the learned transmitted them to Europeans. A similar situation existed among the Celts, and in Ireland oral learning lost its position later, except in the monasteries. It is impossible to tell how archaic the language of the pure pagan texts may have been. After sacred literature – the myths, charms and incantations – the next in importance concerned the law. There can be little doubt that the oral learning of the continental Celts included epic literature and genealogies as well as verse found now within the insular compass of surviving Irish and Welsh literature. In form and style they can be recognized as springing from the common Indo-European heritage.

Select Bibliography

Curtis, E., *A History of Ireland*, London, 1950.

De Paor, M. and L., *Early Christian Ireland*, London, 1958.

Kenny, J. F., *The Sources of the Early History of Ireland*, New York, 1928.

MacNeill, E., *Phases of Irish History and Mythology*, Dublin, 1946.

O'Rahilly, T. F., *Early Irish History and Mythology*, Dublin, 1946.

Wainwright, F. T., *The Problem of the Picts*, Edinburgh, 1955.

You may also enjoy...

The Ancient Picts of the Scottish Highlands of the Seventh Century

♦ *Michael Sheane* ♦